"Every child in the world loves to look up at passing airplanes and marvel at the wonder of air travel. After reading about Betty Greene, young imaginations will look to the skies with gospel possibilities in mind. I hope this book inspires a generation of kids who don't merely want to be pilots but who want to be pilots (or truck drivers or train engineers) for the glory of Christ and the cause of his eternal kingdom."

MEGAN HILL, Editor, The Gospel Coalition; mother of four

"Laura Caputo-Wickham captures timeless truths from Betty Greene's life. Will captivate even the youngest child!"

BARBARA REAOCH, Author, *A Jesus Christmas* and *A Better Than Anything Christmas*

"Courageous, entrepreneurial and bold enough to break through numerous glass ceilings, Betty Greene's passion for the Lord trumped all other barriers to take the gospel to the ends of the earth. She is a truly inspirational role model to us all."

LINDA ALLCOCK, Author, *Head, Heart, Hands* and *Deeper Still*

"Discover how God used a woman with sky-high dreams to bring people across the world to him."

BOB HARTMAN, Author, *The Prisoners, the Earthquake and the Midnight Song*

"The wonderful storytelling and charming illustrations make the mini-biographies in this series pitch-perfect for even the youngest readers."

CHAMP THORNTON, Author, *The Radical Book for Kids*

"A wonderful series, beautifully illustrated, introducing your children to godly women."

BLAIR LINNE, Spoken Word Artist

thegoodbook
for children

Betty Greene
© Laura Caputo-Wickham / The Good Book Company 2021
Illustrated by Héloïse Mab | Design and Art Direction by André Parker
"The Good Book For Children" is an imprint of The Good Book Company Ltd
thegoodbook.com | thegoodbook.co.uk | thegoodbook.com.au
thegoodbook.co.nz | thegoodbook.co.in
ISBN: 9781784986544 | Printed in India

Do Great Things for God

Betty Greene

The Girl Who Longed to Fly

Laura Caputo-Wickham

Illustrated by Héloïse Mab

Betty loved to look at the sky and watch the aeroplanes fly by.

They sparkled in the sun as they soared above her house in Medina, USA.

Betty was the only girl of four children. Playing with her brothers was great fun!

They chased each other across the fields, rode their horse, and listened to the Bible stories that their parents told to the children who lived in their street.

When her big brother, Joe, started flying lessons, Betty watched from down below. She wished that she could learn to fly too.

Then, one Christmas, a kind uncle gave Betty some money.

Betty knew exactly how to spend it.

Flying lessons!

"Wheeee!"

When a big war called World War II started, Betty joined the Women Airforce Service Pilots, also called WASPs. Their job was to help the men during their training.

They even flew with big targets behind their planes for the soldiers to practise on!

After the war, Betty heard of MAF, a new missionary organisation. They wanted to send help and the good news of Jesus to all those places in the world that were hard to get to.

But to do that, they needed brave, enthusiastic pilots.

Enter Betty!

Betty helped MAF to pick their first aeroplane. It was painted bright red. It looked beautiful.

Then the moment came for the very first MAF task: two women needed to be taken to Mexico.

Betty and her two passengers climbed aboard.

The engine roared, the dust rose and everyone waved.

But after a few hours Betty started to worry.
There was something coming out of the engine!

She landed at once and gave the plane a
close look.

With great relief, she realised that the engine
was fine. What she had seen was nothing
more than the red paint of the plane that had
started to peel off!

"Phew!"

Betty flew above the Mexican jungle and looked down at the train tracks snaking through the trees. A journey that would have taken ten hours by train took only two by plane!

As the weeks went by, Betty went on different missions and piloted different planes.

One plane was called the Duck because it could land on water.

One day, Betty was flying the Duck over the Amazon forest when, out of the blue, the engine stopped!

The plane was plummeting down at a very high speed.

They were going to crash!

But just before they crashed, the engine started again, only for a few seconds but long enough for Betty to land on a river.

As she sat there, with the plane safely bobbing on the water, one of her passengers shouted in amazement,

"Señorita, Señorita, why are you so calm?!"

Betty smiled. She knew that God had everything under control.

As she flew above jungles, mountains, seas and deserts, a verse from the Bible came to Betty's mind.

"You will be my witnesses ...
to the ends of the earth."
Acts 1 v 8

Betty looked down and smiled, grateful for being able to do the two things she loved the most—flying and serving her God, the Creator of earth and its big, blue skies.

Betty Greene

1920 Betty—together with her twin brother, Bill—was born in Seattle, USA on the 24th of June. Betty's parents loved Jesus and often shared Bible stories with her and her brothers. They also ran a Sunday school for all the local children.

1927 Betty was only seven years old when pilot Charles Lindbergh become the first man to fly solo across the Atlantic. This sparked an interest in aeroplanes in Betty, which became a real passion when her big brother, Joe, started to take flying lessons. Joe would tell Betty everything he'd learned, and Betty would listen, wishing that one day she too could fly.

1936 A few years later, a generous uncle gave Betty $100. This was a lot of money back then. America was going through a long period of poverty called the Great Depression. Betty used some of the money for things she needed, like clothes and shoes, but the rest went towards flying lessons.

When World War II started, Betty used her skills to serve with the Women Airforce Service Pilots, also known as

WASPs. She even became part of a research project that sent pilots way up high, through the stratosphere!

1944 After WASPs were dissolved, Betty helped to set up a mission called CAMF, which is today known as MAF (Mission Aviation Fellowship).

MAF's goal was to send help to those parts of the world that were isolated or hard to reach.

1946 On February 23rd, 25-year-old Betty took the first MAF flight on a four-seat cabin Waco biplane. After a little hiccup, she arrived safely in the remote Mexican jungle.

This was only the first of many incredible adventures.

Throughout her life, Betty made over 4,640 flights and served in 12 countries, landing in around 20 more.

She was not only the first pilot to fly for MAF but also the first woman to fly over the Andes, the longest mountain range in the world, as well as the first woman to fly a plane to Sudan.

Elizabeth Everts "Betty" Greene

1920 - 1997

"You will be my witnesses ... to the ends of the earth."

Acts 1 v 8

Do Great Things for God

Inspiring biographies for young children

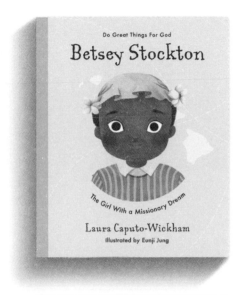

thegoodbook.com | thegoodbook.co.uk